Bright stars of Uzbekistan

MASHKHURA USMANOVA

© Mashkhura Usmanova

Bright stars of Uzbekistan
by: Mashkhura Usmanova
Edition: January '2024
Publisher:
Taemeer Publications LLC (Michigan, USA / Hyderabad, India)

ISBN 978-93-5872-146-1

9 789358 721461

Book	:	Bright stars of Uzbekistan
Author	:	Mashkhura Usmanova
Publisher	:	Taemeer Publications
Year	:	'2024
Pages	:	90
Title Design	:	*Taemeer Web Design*

Farangiz Murodova Asliddin's daughter was born on September 25, 2004 in Gallaorol district, Jizzakh region. Currently, she is a first-year student of the Uzbek language and literature department of the Bukhara State Pedagogical Institute.

"The waves like the sea are
From age of love"
(Fakhriyor)

Falling in love in a person's life,
 Thought it was just happiness.
Sometimes these eyes stare,
I thought it was from deep excitement.

Let me read your love story,
I would like it to be such a miracle.
Let him prove his truth,
When I say don't die, "I have" a song.

Why did you trust your age?
Even the rays in the eyes are gone.
Do you need to suffer so much?
You are better than this situation.

A single drop that fell from my lips,
Salt water in the same container.
Did you find someone to help you?
Chase for yourself if you are not yourself.

Sometimes youth comes from an invisible heart,
Our hearts are somewhat sleepy in old age.
Hear your voice from the false sky,
Then the salty soil will press your body...

On January 12, 2007, **Gozal Sunnatova** daughter of **Shuhrat**, became a member of the "Qaqnus" club of "Barkamol avlod" children's school, Gallaorol district, Jizzakh region. Currently, she is 10th grade student of school 44.

The last poem…
I couldn't write a single line of poetry,
My heart was pounding for a long time.
Inspiration never fails,
It is a deal I made invain.

My troughts are very confused,
The heart does not know what to do.
Mind command me:
"You must arrive tomorrow"

But I never understood myself,
I couldn't see any way out of the dilemma.
When I told him cry, he cried too late,
My eyes are dry with tears.

I have no feelings left in my heart,
The dark night kills me.
I am just desperate now,
I live for the end…

Khasanova is the daughter of **Dilobarkhan Abdumannab**. She was born on August 29, 2003 in the Shahrikhan district of Andijan region. She is currently a 2nd - year student of the Department of Sociology at the Faculty of History of Fergana State University.

Concept and essence of content analysis method in sociology

Annotation:
The method and methodology of sociological research is the main branch of the science of Sociology, in it, debates such as research work, program creation, and problem solving are related to this science. One of them is the content analysis method, which is considered the main method. We will focus on the main essence and structure of the method, its interaction with other sciences, and how important it is for researchers to study and use this method more widely.
Keywords: Content, research, context, method, subject, conceptual, gender, thinking, category, policy.

We know that every science has its own common features and aspects. Knowledge, skills are all related to different terms. Today, total concepts rely on basic methods. The main method of research in sociology in content analysis. What is content analysis? Sociologists have provided basic information on this question. Content analysis, translated from English as "content", is the main standard research method in the field of social sciences, and the analysis method is the content of arrays and communicative correspondence. Researchers can draw broader conclusions by studying word usage in context. Content analysis is a research method used by sociologists to analyze social life by interpreting words and images from documents, films, art, music, and other cultural products and mass media. They study the concepts related to the main culture depending on the applied context, especially their interactions. Content analysis can help researchers to study the areas of socialism that are difficult to analyze, such as gender issues, business strategy and policy, human resources, and the theory of the organization. It is widely used to research the place. For example, in advertising, female subjects are usually depicted in relation to men by their lower physical position or the arousing nature of their passions or gestures. Types of content analysis method researchers now different recognize content analysis they get each of them covers a different approach. According to a report published in the Journal of Medical Health Quality of Life Research, there are 3 different types:

1. Traditional
2. Directed
3. Total

In traditional content analysis, coding categories are derived directly from the text. Analysis with a planned approach begins with theories as a guide to initial codes. Aggregate content analysis usually involves counting and comparing keywords or content. Other experts write about the difference between conceptual analysis and relational analysis. Conceptual analysis not only determines how often certain words or phrases of a text are used, but also how these words and phrases relate to certain broader concepts. Conceptual analysis is traditionally s from of content analysis. Usually, the questions that researchers want to answer through content analysis are to identify. The term content analysis was first used in the late 19th and early 20th centuries. In American journalism (see B. Matthews, A. Tenney, D. Speed, D. Wipkins). The origin of the methodology of content analysis is the American sociologist G. Lasswell and the French journalist J. Kaiser was. Advantages of content Analysis content analysis has a number of significant advantages over other methods, and simply obvious advantages.

Among them, the following should be noted: it directly studies communication itself through text analysis, which allows the researcher to interact with the main means of communication in society. Works with qualitative and quantitative data. Descriptive can provide valuable historical/cultural information Presentation [text] allows to obtain information close to, although the degree of such similarity varies depending on the tools used Can be used to analyze the desired material as a tool for developing specific systems "inconspicuous" method [in this case, the participants of communication do not experience any discomfort during the analysis, because the method does not directly interfere with communication] it takes a comprehensive, holistic and language. When is used, it is considered objective discursive unlike analysis, real facts. Units of content analysis after determining the system of analysis categories, the appropriate unit of text analysis is selected. Bogomolova N.N and Stefanenko T.G suggest sharing that content analysis units are divided into two large groups.

- Quality

Qualitative units of content analysis answer the question of WHAT should be counted in the text, and quantitative units answer the question of HOW to count. To suggests defining categories and their referents (indicators) in the qualitative text. It should note that different terms are used to designate different units of content analysis – the category- is recognized by all authors. The large inconsistency in terminology when referring to different units of content analysis makes the procedure somewhat difficult to understand. This is the method. Categories can be divided into smaller qualitative units- subcategories. Indicators categories are those elements of the adjective of

7

related categories and subcategories. Depending on the specific characteristics of learning, category indicators can be expressed in the from of individual words, phrases, sentences, topics, etc.

References:

1. Sociological encyclopedia. Under total ed. A.N. Danilova. Minsk, 2003
2. Dridze T.M text activity in the context of social communication. M, 1984
3. Methodological and methodical problems of content analysis. Edition. 1-2. M, 1973
4. Methods of document analysis in sociological research. M, 1985
5. Effectiveness of mass media. M, 1986

Kazakhova Sarvinoz Jahangir's daughter was born on November 23, 1997. She is student of Gulistan State University. Her work has appeared in several international collections.

Come on!

Come! Check it out! My eyes,
Become a wonder in my eyes.
Bubbling in my marrow,
Place yourself in the bed of longing love.
And my beautiful feelings,
With your reviving breath,
My dashed hopes,
Get together with your cage.
Make my heart crazy
Wake up my slumbering past.
There are few fools like me,
May you laugh at the love of Layli.
I have a flying bird in my veins,
Your are full of yellow leaves.
Landing slowly in my place,
My dry pains are gone.
Come! Come! White as the mornings,
Untie the chains of my longing.
Dust without our body,
It's late for a thousand years!
Come on! Let's go

Mashhura Abduhalilova Akmal's daughter eas born in 2009. 7th grade student of school 24, Gallaorol district, Jizzakh region. Member of the "Qaqnus" club at the "Barkamol avlod" children's school.

Mother

I kept hurting your heart,
You wished if I could tell you one warm word.
Mother, I shedded your tears vainly,
I did not appreciate you the way you deserve.

From today, I made a strong covenant to myself,
I realized you are the biggest happiness I have.
Throughout all this time, years chasing each other,
Mother, I want you to be finally happy with your children's love

.

The daughter of **Dinora Khamraqulova Jumanazar** was born in 2005. 11th grade student of school 18, Kasbi district, Kashkadarya province. Young reader few winner and young union leader.

Is the Tutor good or the School?

Nowadays, many people think that it is more effective for young people to learn in tutor than in school. At the moment, both teachers and students are of the same opinion. The reason is that a significant part of the students who entered the university are those who education from tutors.

Well, for those of you who ask, what's up with that? This is a sad situation for our society. For example, if 50 graduates from one school entered the university, 45 of them entered because of additional education outside the school. Should we then conclude that school education is not enough to enter a university? Those questions in the exam are made from school textbooks. Students lose confidence and respect for school education. He attends classes inattentively or begins to skip classes. His main attention is occupied with the tasks of his teacher, who is teaching him outside the classroom. In fact, most tutors are school teachers. They can also conduct free science clubs for students at school. But for some reason they don't...

True, there are dedicated teachers who give free lessons at school. But unfortunately, they are few in number.

Talking about the quality of education makes some teachers cringe. But it must be admitted that this issue is the most urgent now. Many people may not know that it is the most effective method to encourage the student in the lesson. As a student, I would like to express this opinion. It is clear that a student without interest will not want to study. If the teacher is not interested in science, if the parents lose hope without support, the student will turn out to be more ignorant than any school. And the tutors will explain the lessons with strict control and encouragement. If a teacher doesn't like his work, he can't make the lesson interesting. If parents are indifferent to their child's future, they will not control their child's education.

The tutor simply repeats the lessons and topics learned at school and replaces them in the student's mind. Before that, the student did not spend more than an hour on a topic recommended by the tutor, even if he had previously written it in his notebook. If he had taken the time, he would not have felt the need for a tutor.

My conclusion is that school education is free. Tutor education is paid. Choosing one of the two is up to the student and his parents.

Munisa Eshmo'minova Nurali daughter was born 9th July, 2003 in Kashkadarya, Karshi city, in Otchopar street. She began her studying at 44th school in Karshi, then she entered to World State University of foreign Languages as a grant student. She is a know English, Turkish language.

Kind Mother

Not even if the moon isn't smiling into the sky,
Not even if the stars cover up the sky.
Boston is my pearl,
My mother is kind and alone in the world.

While the blossoms are blooming one after the other,
The world is filled with love.
I'm the one in the world,
My mother is one of the seven wonders.

Spring is not spreading its freshness,
Girls don't open their flower faces.
My hope in all this world,
Spring refreshes the darling mother.

If inspiration does not come to poets,
The wind play with his hair.
My enchanting time, full of light and pleasure,
You are my true angel, good mother.

The daughter of **Ra'no Bobomurodova Bakhtiyar** was born on in 2007. 10th grade student of school 25, Gallaorol district, Jizzakh region. Member of "Qaqnus" club at "Barkamol avlod" children's school.

Unbookish children

Every nation wants its offspring,
To be educated.
They will surely reach perfection if,
They read a lot of books.

Somehow, today, in our time,
Not everyone likes reading.
We do not have interests in,
Becoming better generations.

The technologies became the global,
Global problems of the world.
If we were book readers,
We would have deffinately solved it.
Let's read more often,
Let's make our minds think broadly.
Let's make our parents proud,
Of what we have achieved.

Isheryakova Joanna Rinat daughter was born on January 26, 2004 in Russia. Nowadays, she is a second year student of Foreign Languages Faculty of Bukhara State University. Winner of the contest "Student of Year 2022".

And a mother's heart

And a mother's heart is one,
Cries and sobs with you.
And we are not given that understanding,
How mothers sometimes suffer for us.

And a mother's heart is the only answer,
To all questions, the mysteries of all life.
And do not forget us that wise advise,
What did the mother give in the Motherland- Fatherland.

And the mother's heart, when you are far away-
It is like a compass correct and accurate,
And you walk briskly, lightly-
At will show your immaculate path.
And the mother's heart keeps from all sorrows,
It always goes with you and is indivisible.
Watch it carelessly, don't break it,
It is forever one, unique.

And a mother's heart is the most honest of all,
It always wishes us good luck.
With his love, success awaits in everything,
Hurry to comfort when mom is crying.

But sometimes you will pass with a chill,
You don't notice the pain in your heart at all.
Remember: a mother's heart is one,
You are responsible for it in front of God!

Sheraliyeva Feruza Muhammadjon daughter was born in 2005 in Muzrabot district of Alpomish neighborhood of Surkhandarya region. Currently, she is a 10th grade student at 55th school in this area. She is actively attending in the essay competition "Constitution is the foundation of our happiness".

Corruption is the evil of development

There are various types of corruption in the world. Thousands of studies have been conducted by scientists, various institutions and international organizations to reveal the reasons for its origin, to find effective ways to combat it. The work and researches in this regard are continuing consistently. What is corruption itself? Who will carry it out? How does corruption arise? Problematic questions, which were mentioned above, encountered in our society. So what is corruption itself? Who are its true essence and the forces that drive it?

The term corruption is commonly used to refer to the political apparatus. Buying officials, their sale of bribes are also called corruption. The most common types of corruption include bribery, fraud, extortion and nepotism. The word "corruption" in Latin means violation and nausea. After the independence of our country was announced, a number of normative legal acts were adopted aimed at preventing crime. Although the state agencies which fight against corruption were established, they are not working hard enough solve the problem. Literally, the amount of corruption is increasing day by day. And the worst side is that people are indifferent to such state, treat it as a normal condition.

If we take a deeper look at corruption and the associated economic crime in today's economic and political situation of states, it is considered to be the main source of

16

danger that hinders progress and one of the main threats to security. The scale of damage that were taken as a consequence of corruption is endless.

Every citizen who aims to have stable conditions for honest work, spending knowledge, energy, creative abilities, and who wants his or her children and loved ones to enjoy the results of civilized market relations in democratic and civil society in the future, should put a necessary barrier on the path of corruption in time. I reckon that majority of individuals have well understood what sad consequence these vices may have.

We need to fight against the scourge of corruption together, with tact and bold steps. Each law is adopted with a noble purpose, seeking positive outcomes. A closer acquaintance with the law, an attempt to apply it to our life, understanding of how terrible the scourge of corruption is, an independent perception, and most importantly, the fight against it is the civic duty of each of person.

Inobat Karimova Umidbek daughter was born on December 28, in 2000 in Khorezm region. Currently, she is a student of the 2nd level in Karshi. She is very interested in poetry, literature and painting. In the future, she want to become a great poetess and beloved teacher.

It's raining
Why are you shedding tears?
Tell me if you miss my breasts.
Or do you have something to say,
It's like you're writing some words.

If you cry, I feel sad, my dear,
It's as your tears are coming to hearts.
I've been waiting for the rain for a long time here,
Pain of longing fills my hearts.

Tell me, where did you come from, rain?
Is she peaceful in distant lands?
Tell me if you're tired,
In the places where you have walked.

Tell me if you have met with her,
Sweet times happened in the past.
Or you turned back without seeing,
Wasn't she on those roads?
Feel revenge her from others,
I will set myself on fire.
Who do I want to contact now?
If you can't find it either.

If rain drops talk about you,
I wish I could listen to all of them.

Every drop without putting it on the ground with you,
If I understand the secret of your heartache.

Rain, I have one word from you,
Tell my hot love to her.
Before the rain turns to ice,
The pain of my love don't she hear?

A moment of peace with the words of rain,
My heart finds comfort with it.
I'm still waiting for her to come,
It's hard if I can reach it.

Rain, I have many words for you,
Let her know if you can deliver.
Whisper softly my love to her,
Come back with your answer.

Intizor Samandarova Ikromjon daughter was born on May 3, 2007 in Gurlen district, Khorezm region. She is young poetess and writer. In 2022, a collection of poems entitled "The Best Invitation" was published. She is member of international organizations.

Uzbekistan

Independence gave us a wide opportunity,
Today, people look to the future.
A country that is reborn and shining,
In the new Uzbekistan, people are dear.

The third renaissance is taking root,
Every field is developing further.
Pays a lot of attention to education,
In the new Uzbekistan, people are dear.

Dear president of my dear country,
He supports us as a helper.
He turns to the people and says:
In the new Uzbekistan, people are dear.

New buildings are popping up every day,
Ibn Sina, Navai, Babur Mirza are born again.
We are the pride, love and honor of the Motherland,
In the new Uzbekistan, people are dear.
This is a place where human dignity is glorified,
Young people are concentrated in one point.
Is this year's slogan,
In new Uzbekistan, people are dear.

Steps towards to future,
Everyone is happy today.
May your part be bright, may the sky be clear,
In the new Uzbekistan, people are dear, people are dear!

Zarnigor Ubaidullayeva Ilhomjon's daughter was born on January 29, 2005 in Gallaorol district, Jizzakh region. Currently, a student of the 11th grade at school 54th

A place where spring has turned into dreams
The white look of the morning in my window,
The sun of my heart rises from afar.
There is beauty in this world,
Spring is on such a fire.

The place where tulips bloom on the shores,
This world will be more beautiful.
Wake up early, look at the trees,
Spring is on such a fire.
Spring is quiet in the bosom of dreams,
There are moonlit nights.
When I open my eyes everything is bright,
A place where spring has turned into dreams.

Marhabo Suyunova Murod's daughter was born on June 22, 2001 in Guzor district, Kashkadaryo region the Republic of Uzbekistan. Currently, Marhabo is a student of the Faculty of English Philology at Karshi State University.

Wish is
This is world river eyes age share,
This is world river connect fulfillment share.
One person recover quiet days,
This world sad beating from share.

Blossom just face as moon filled,
New century joyful century share filled.
Every tulip nooks and plant itself,
Every bird someone is field itself.

This world put at position enjoy,
There is exist person finally child.
Centuries radiant century share filled,
New century share freedom filled.

Yoldosheva Madinabonu Kahraman's daughter was born on January 7, 2004 in Gallaorol district, Jizzakh region. Currently, Madinabonu is a student of the 2nd stage evening education faculty of the Jizzakh State Pedagogical University.

In memory of Zulfiyakhanim

When the spring has arrived in every tree and in every sprout,
The flowers bloom seeking your name.
As it is familiar to them, it is to me too,
The way of life you lived and put steps to.

You are the light, the name of affection is fervent,
This is the prove that you're in love with your Khamid.
Even if it is not you, but your spirit is alive,
Amorous heart is always alive.

And your poems, they are too, written out of love,
Each line is an inspiration of that very love.
The inspiration to your poems to your life-
Look, the peach has bloomed again.

Your poem heart is so spotless just like the sky,
So many hearts still cannot forget it.
Every word you wrote ignited my heart,
My poems and the off spring of your love.

Meyliyeva Zebiniso Mirkomil daughter was born on June 4, 2003 in Kashkadarya region. In 2010-2021, she studied at school 61. Currently, Zebiniso is a student at the Faculty of Social Sciences of the National University of Uzbekistan named after Mirzo Ulugbek, on the basis of a state grant.

Thank you teacher
My dear person,
My dear teacher.
Like a white bird,
You gave a big life.

We fly to the each side,
Pray for us my teacher.
You can trust me,
I'm getting your student girl.

My kind teacher,
My scholar- intellectual.
My dear teacher,
Be happy and stay safe.

I thank you, teacher
You gave me education.
Your work is inspiration,
I will be a scientist, a doctor.
As soon as possible,
You can trust me,
I will be a good student,
You are proud of me.

Pulatova Hulkaroy Olimjan daughter was born on June 24, 2007 in Samarqand region. Currently, Hulkaroy is a student of the 9 "A" grade of the creative school named after Erkin Vahidov, Fergana region.

Isn't technology made people lazy?!

Life... Time... Technology age... Development... If put the word "technology" on one side of the issue, and the concept of "human labor" on the other side. So which one is heavier? See, the creation of technology is also permeated by the tireless work, research and research of man. How do you explain the concept of "human labor" in the second step?

After centuries of non-stop activity, does a person become more prone to laziness? It's up to the person to develop or change, change and change their own work! Do you support this idea?

Let's think about this for a moment. After a person was born, in this bright world, his self-thought developed, he began to fight for himself, for living, after so much hard work, wars and developments, person reached this level. For centuries, he struggles with himself, the biggest obstacle in this bright world. He overcame his fear. He gave up when he was about to succeed. As if that wasn't enough, he decided to start all over again! He got up, limped, straightened, started and ran. Ana ran with that incomparable enthusiasm and speed and entered the era called "Age of Progress". The development of this time was created by man with his own hands, mind and thinking. Man realized that he could make unprecedented changes. He used his inventions for development. He studied the universe. He was interested in nature, the environment, human health, animals, the history of our planet and the planets, the emergence and development of man, in short, everything. He made inventions that develop man, he made universal discoveries that completely destroy human development. Do you see? Man's mind and thinking are limitless, man was created to be rich in every way. Now let's look at the events of the 21st century.

- It was difficult for those who thought that money would solve all problems.
- Conscious. Mature people often find simplistic concepts acceptable. I realized that opportunities often come in the form of failures and temporary setbacks.

Universal made its discoveries and inventions through these concepts. Rivals and competitors came into the circle in terms of production, technologies, industrial development. You see, 100% of people try to leave 90% halfway. Since he could not create anything new, he began to take revenge for the inventions that brought the great to the level of greatness.

After that, only 10% of people provide the world with technology through their own work and efforts. 45% of people still plan to study without learning these methods. The remaining 45% of the population buy these modern technologies and use them for their own benefit.

Now let's analyze the most important aspect of our topic and the reason for the discussion! "Doesn't technology make people lazy?"

- People are losing their personal opinions and conclusions.
- Through social networks, young students imitate other people and lose their identity.
- Mathematical processes are performed not mentally, but through a simple calculator installed on a mobile phone.
- Human capital has decreased, so that human hands that previously produced large

productions are now idle, creating unemployment in the right places.

- Damage to the environment, water and sea pollution is associated with increased energy consumption of many industries.
- Social networks- they disrupt the social life of many students. They spend more time playing games or developing apps on mobile devices.
- Apathy and laziness will increase in the world as processes become faster and more efficient, making every activity easier.

We are enjoying our fullness now. A phone in the hands of a 2-year-old child who does not even understand anything yet. Students who have just entered the 1st grade talk with their friends not about textbooks, but about the game "PUGB" and where the world's fantastic films are. Where is the enlightenment here? Before, during the time of the former Shura, reading one book was a hundred thousand hardship. In the 14th and 15th centuries, only officials, not ordinary people, could enter large libraries. But why such a system is bad, enlightened people, intellectuals who surprised, intellectuals who surprised the world even in time of suffering of the people grew up. Were there telephones then? TV, internet, wife, washing machines, touch devices, modern equipment in the field of medicine? Was there are there e-audio books, Google, chrome, you tube, tik tok, facebook platforms and sites? Is there such a peaceful, satisfying, abundant, great opportunity? No, no and no again. People of that life we live. They sacrificed their lives to create such an era for us, for the future generation. What about us? What are we doing for our ancestors, not to mention them, for our parents, for our own future? Tell me, what are we doing? Is there a person among us who considers himself wise, enlightened, intelligent? Tell me! We can't even keep our promise to ourselves! Our resolve is weakening day by day. We don't even... do it in the morning prayer. We lie under a warm blanket with sweet sleep.

Do you know? Why the great were great! Our famous veterans also appeared during the war years. He considered the words fatigue, laziness, sleep, rest to be completely foreign to them. He worked while everyone was sleeping, he was able to stick to his ideas, he worked on himself when people started working. When ordinary people were looking for a ladder to their success, they created this ladder with their hard work and dreams. Neither you nor he was as prepared as we were. Imagine... someone in the newspaper covered this news in the form of an article. Next to it, a funny, interesting, video came to your phone from some platform. You completely forget about the newspaper. You become addicted to the phone and get lost in the world that drives you crazy.

You go to the library, take a book and watch a series instead of reading, is that so? No, no. Don't fool yourself. Don't be fooled either. Or have you not been in this situation at all?! Admit it, there will be times when the library will go down to level 2 for you.

Uh...people...uh...time...

Times flies! You liked the video that arrived on your phone for a few minutes. Look, it's temporary. Your streak is over. What will happen now?! Is your wallet full of 10 million?! Has a new building been built in front of your house?! Have you become a world famous businessman and billionaire? No, if you spend your phone time on newspaper news, spend your TV time on reading a book, even 1% will change your life. If I am wrong, try to interpret your own life. It is better to suffer the bitter truth and change yourself for the better than to be drink seconds, on a sweet lie. If my words are harsh, if you think that my opinion is wrong, then you yourself know. It's just the little things that make our lives flourish and liven up, but ignoring them can lead us to the brink. Is it worth it to find and copy information from Google in 5 seconds, or is it worth it to find it in 5-6 books? Of course, the time and effort we put into writing is valuable. We can stay away from social networks and read 200 books a year. If we stay away from the artificial technologies around us for 1 week and spend time in nature, our body will recover 90% by itself. The biggest risk factors for our health are 95% technology and the other 5% our attention. My dears!!! There is a lot to say. I think you understand the rest! I'm not saying technology is useless. They are an integral part of our life. Everything depends on us, our actions, our determination. Time is just passing, life is passing. We cannot change the past. As soon as we know that we have a tendency to various vices, let us fight against it. If you find the cause of your laziness in other ways and get used to your life, you will consider your life wasted. Your life is in your hands. Don't change the world or the technology. Just change yourself. Then live. Then you will understand what real human actions are! The conclusion is from yourself.

Aydin Rakhmatullayeva Ravshan daughter was born in Kaprin village, Guzor district, Kashkadarya reagion. Currently, he is working as a student of Uzbek language and literature at TAFU and as an ambulance worker of Guzor district.

***

The importance isn't our presence,
And don't say- if I die, the world will feel sadness.
The sun will shine even after us,
You should know it's a truth.

Don't talk! Your words remain in the mouth,
Suddenly you can't find anything it is truth,
Blue garden, this world is not forever,
Just like the ones you had a dream about ever.

Don't think..! Because of unaccustomed arrogance,
Don't get used to being silent always.
Just don't ask you to stay away,
Somebody think she is alive far away.

Don't search..! There is no way, no solution,
Your dress is a shroud, your house is a coffin.
If you can't find a solution, don't be hurrying kindly,
You know the end of the address is dirt surely.
Maybe our existence is unknown in this...
Maybe our absence doesn't matter in this...

Zaripova Muborak Zubaydullo's daughter was born on September 30, 2008 in Kagan district of Bukhara region of the Republic of Uzbekistan. Currently, she is studying at the 1st school of the state national economy in the Kagan distict of Bukhara.

Is connecting to the phone a new type of disease?

Technologies become an integral part of our different faces close, the techniques that have become the machine of our household, smart phones and televisions have become the meaning of our lives. Vehicles close our reach, and alternatively the poisonous fumes emanating from them poison nature, people, causing various diseases. We observe the world by TV, but the rays emanating from them cause eye diseases. The phone is you-it has become our everyday companion. Their importance is very great. We will be aware of World News through phones, we find ourselves looking for the information we need. But affection is disappearing among people through phones. There are not a few individuals suffering from various diseases as a result of using the phone for a bad purpose, getting attached to it. The rays and waves emanating from the phone damage the internal organs of person. The psychological effects of mobile phones have not been scientifically proven that it harms health. It is the highest wealth for a person, and it is necessary to use the phone in moderation for our health.

Internet is a big supermarket. Everyone buys what they need. Of course, there are many people who use the internet for the right purpose. But most people don't spend their time usefully because they follow people's profiles. For example: different picture or meals and others. Young people are becoming wild by playing various entertaining games on the internet while wasting their lives in the period of learning. Being attached to the phone has reached the level of "disease" today. It must be used only and only for reasonable purposes.

Mashhura Usmonova Zafarjon's daughter was born on May 16, 2006 in Gallaorol district, Jizzakh region. In addition, her works have been published in book collections of the United States of America, Turkey, British and un Azerbaijan.

The first step
Parents are so happy today,
Because their daughter has put her first steps.
Maybe the Father is even happier,
He has felt the real happiness of life.

Mother feels on the cloud nine,
The world is narrow for their happiness.
The laughter has not stopped today at all,
It is like, no one is happier than they are.

When I put my first steps towards you,
Did you have the same pleasure?
Without fitting into the world,
Were you happy, tell me poetry?

Husenova Maryam Hamza daughter in Kagan district of the Bukhara region.

I study at school.
***

Unusual contrast is seen in your world,
Unusual emotion comes from it indeed.
This emotion is called as peace,
If you're in peace, nothing is in need.

You are worth for a great name today,
  For the name of prosperous land.
Achieving your goals these days,
Coming to the light from those dark days.

You're also a develop country,
Smiling to a new life again.
My country, you're flourishing forever,
Making my nation's dreams true.

Gold is hidden under patience,
Shining over the sky again and again.
Your peace us forever alive,
Standing over all difficulties.

This day was a dream of Chulpan,
It was precious to Behbudiy too.
Kadiri gave his life for education,
Avloni stood for literature.

Muminova Mukhlisa Farhad's daughter was born on February 11, 2007 in Jizzakh district of jizzakh region. Currently, she is a 9th grade student in 8th general secondary school in Jizzakh.

Two geniuses of a century
                    "There is nowhere such a rich history as in our motherland,
such great scholars as our ancestors"

(Shavkat Mirziyoyev)
By studying the creative works of two great figures in the history of Uzbek classical literature – Alisher Navoi and Zahiriddin Muhammad Babur, we can get enough idea of what a truly human life should be like.

Alisher Navoi is one of the great figure in the history of Uzbek literature and culture. His contemporaries glorified him as "Nizamiddin Mir Alisher". "Nizamiddin"- means the charter of region. Navoi was born on February 9, 1441 in the capital of Khorasan state – the park of the city of Herat on the territory of present day Afghanistan on the theme of the state House. His father, Giyosiddin Muhammad, served in the Timuri Palace, was one of the influential people of his time and paid serious attention to the upbringing, education of Navoi.

Alisher Navoi wrote perfect poems in two languages. In the Turkish language, he used the pseudonyms "Navoi", and in the Persian language - "Foniy". The poetic heritage of Alisher Navoi, created in the Uzbek language, is mainly collected in the selection of "Xazoyin ul-maoniy". Navoi wrote the creative work "Muhokamat ul-lug'atayn" and restored the historical prestige of the Turkish language. In this invaluable work, he talks about the phenomenon of the Turkish language, talks about the wealth of Turkish folklore and ethnography, snows the internal capabilities and advantages of the Turkish language. In the 1500s, the life conditions of the poet became more difficult. His health obviously deteriorated, but he didn't stop writing poems. On January 3, 1501, Navoi died as a consequence of severe illness. The entire Herat people mourned for seven days for their great poet.

And Zahiriddin Muhammad Babur is a major statesman and commander, along with being a writer, poet, scientist, who occupies a special place in medieval eastern culture, literature and poetry. Babur was born on February 14, 1483 in Andijan in the family of Omar Sheikh Mirzo, governor of Fergana valley. Fond of literature, exquisite art, beauty of nature from an early age, Babur, like all Timurian princes, took the basis of these sciences under the guidance of mature teachers in his father's palace.

With a broad outlook and excellent intelligence, Babur founded the Baburiy dynasty in India and left his name as a statesman in the history of this country, also ranked among the world's historical graphical scholars with his fabulous work "Baburnoma", the aspects and qualities inherent in the peoples of Central Asia, Afghanistan and India, along with the breadth and complexity of their thinking world, are manifested in the problems of life of that time, a complete picture of political and social life in the state, which was organized by Babur. In addition to his lyric poems historical "Baburnoma", Babur also created works in Islamic law and other fields. Babur died in Agra in December 1530, and later, according to his last will, his children brought his grave to Kabul and buried him.

As a historian, lyric poet and scientist, who contributed to the solution of social issues with his known and famous works, Babur occupies a worthy place in the history of the spiritual culture of our people.

Alisher Navoi and Zahiriddin Muhammad Babur are two bright stars that illuminate Uzbek classical literature. It is

36

no wonder that they are contemporaries, who live in one century and it is the great wisdom of the creator.

I remember... at the age of four of five, my teacher gave four lines of poetry to memorize. I that was the poem of Navoi:

That will be no strange joy in pride,
Nor will the people be kind to him.
Inside the golden cage if a red flower grows,
It tortures a nightingale like a thorn.

Still these lines sound in my ear. As I move to high school, my interest in the creative works of Alisher Navoi and Babur, the contribution of these two geniuses, who shook the whole world with a pen, to our language and literature is growing.

Then I ask myself the question that Navoi, who knew more than fifty thousand verses by heart, even his mentor Mavlono Lutfi, writes that he wants to replace all his life's work with the following one verse of creativity to twelve thousand verses of poems.

"Every moment when you close your face tears will pour in my eyes,
I think the star will appear, when the sun will rise".

I am proud that I was born in the land of such great geniuses. I encourage their creativity to be perfectly studied by my peers and future generations. As a young creative person, I also try to continue writing for the sake of two great geniuses. I write poems and articles and publish them in newspapers and magazines of our Republic. Every year in February, festive events and literary evenings are held throughout the Republic, dedicated to the birthdays of these two geniuses. Continuing this tradition, I wrote an article with the aim of pleasing their spirits. My dear grandparents, your creativity will never die and will live for thousands more years! New readers will enjoy your creativity.

Sirojiddin Karim (Turdiyev) was born on January 15, 1989 in the village Qorongul, Gallaorol district, Jizzakh region. In 2020, he was admitted to the Writer's union of Uzbekistan.

Mountains

I will never ever forget that,
We once climbed with you together.
Right now I became without you,
And the mountains are my listener.

Unfortunately, my dreams drowned,
To the old sea called sorrow.
I am over thinking and by my thoughts,
Those mountains are always passed though.

We always would climb together,
Thanks to the wings of dreams.
It wasn't excruciating to reach the top,
Now it is a real pain to look at mountains.

Mountains remind you of all times,
When I look at them, my soul is depressed.
So that I can forget you, darling,
Those mountains must be collapsed.

Charos Isomiddinova was born on October 27, 2007 in the Samarkand city, the republic of Uzbekistan. A member of Asih Sasami of Indonesia, Juntos por las letras writers union of Argentina, Iqra foundation of Pakistan.

Sun

The sun gives the coin pleasure,
Softness to the heart, strength.
There are tulips in the sun,
Children running in the sun.
Flowers see the sun,
They will be happy.
The sun is so kind,
Sweet bread in the oven.

Spring

Look at the gentle breeze,
It is blowing in a wide field.
Cut the tulip fields,
You will meet everywhere.

Filling ditches,
The water flows noisily.
Flowers by the roadside,
Smile at him.

Jumamurodova Gullola Bakhtiyor daughter was born in 2003 in Bukhara region of Uzbekistan. She is study Chirchik pedagogical university Gullola Sunshine MUN2 delegate. He is a member of the National Human Rights and Humanitarian Federations and a children's consultant of the Glory Future Foundation.

Highly spiritual generation-creators of the Third Renaissance

Abstract

The issue of educating our youth, who are the future of our country, as all-around successful, educated, competent and perfect human beings, is being approached today in a unique way, on the basis of modern methods, and the organizational and legal foundations are up-to-date to protect all their rights and freedoms, opportunities and interests. Is improving in sync with after all, today's youth is the future of the country, the foundation for its development. That is why the youth is recognized as an active layer of society at all times.

Keywords: intellectual youth, Third renaissance, future, new Uzbekistan.

Introduction

"We set ourselves the main goal of creating the foundation of a new Renaissance, that is, the Third renaissance, in Uzbekistan through large-scale democratic changes, including educational reforms. Speaking of this, first of all, the third Each of us, our whole society, should deeply understand the essence of the Renaissance.

If we look at history, we can see that our motherland, located at the intersection of the Great Silk Road, has been one of the centers of high civilization and culture since time immemorial. The rich scientific and cultural heritage of our people, ancient stone inscriptions, priceless architectural monuments, rare inscriptions, various antiques testify to the deep roots of our statehood history of three thousand years", says Shavkat Mirziyoyev.

Methodology
The young generation is the tomorrow of the country's future, the key to its development.
This is the first foundation that was laid. That is why Uzbekistan looks to the young generation with eyes of hope. They are the initiators of the third renaissance. The role of young people was incomparable in the period of the Eastern Renaissance, in the activities of the moderns, and in the renewal of society. The young generation is the one who develops the country. Is considered an active layer. In this respect, this layer, which is formed regularly, requires constant guidance and support...
The ancient world is a witness that the world has always been governed by ideas. Ideas have always relied on knowledge, thinking and the power of reason. In today's era of rapid development, the horizons of science are expanding, moreover, in the era of the development of information tools, the struggle for idea is sure to require some complications and acute comfort. However, according to its nature, humanity still feels the need for a noble idea. In this sense, one can understand such a great goodness and a great power in the phrase "Third Renaissance" that is written in the history of Uzbekistan today. After all, renaissance means awakening. That is, scientific awakening understanding of enlightenment, and at the same time passing years equal to centuries in moments. Few people are lucky enough to start this process and lay its foundations. It is necessary to embody the nation and sincere humanitarianism in a person.
Today we are living in such a blessed time, in the time when the foundations of the Third renaissance are being

laid in the holy land known to the world as the new Uzbekistan. The youth of new Uzbekistan is the foundation of our future and perspective. The idea of the third renaissance is extremely wonderful. The reason is that in today's science-based era, when the world can be controlled only by science, only such ideas can gain powerful power.

The fact that our president sees the future of our country in education and science, that the idea of the third renaissance has risen to the level of a national idea, and in his desire to face the modern world and be on par with the world, one can see another glimmer of this sense of the Motherland and nation. This feeling is shared by the thirst for enlightenment that is burning in the blood of our people and the longing for the great renaissance paintings of the distant past. Therefore, this nation has a thousand times right to fill the world stage with a new civilization.

Such great goals are embodied in today's great ideas, which serve as the slid foundations of the third renaissance.

In the idea of established the foundations of the third renaissance in Uzbekistan, which was put forward by the head of our state, the involvement of the young generation in science was specifically mentioned. That is why young people were defined as "the main drivers" in achieving this goal. Wide opportunities are being created, a system is being formed to encourage young people in science and enlightenment, and to appreciate, and to appreciate those who have knowledge. In turn, young people should be able to find sources of motivation for their personal development- be it books, libraries, sports or travel let it be. We must all work together to expand the number of young men and women who do not say that they will study when the opportunity arises, but who say that they will try to learn and develop in any situation. In this holy

42

land where we live, when the Awakening- Renaissance begins most of us probably know that Europe is still in a state of heedlessness. Today, wide opportunities have been created, and the motivational words of our country's president are inspiring us. The youth of the third renaissance must have intellectual potential. Today, young people with intellectual potential are the hope for the entire nation, the entire state, and the entire future. The spark is scattered across the ground.

It should also be mentioned that as a result of the wide-ranging campaigning activities carried out in our country on the basis of the idea of "from national revival to national rise", the self-thinking and world view of our people have changed. The noble idea of "New Uzbekistan" which has become a nationwide movement, has finally decided to create foundations of the third renaissance based on the spiritual maturity of the individual. Fundamental reforms in many areas, such as storage, are the foundation atones of the third renaissance. The third renaissance serves to increase the pace of creation and strengthen the ideological immunity of the population.

Conclusion

At the end of my speech, I would like to say that, first of all, our society should deeply understand the idea of the third renaissance. Our work in every front, in every field, our plans and perspective programs, education and personnel policy, investment policy- all are conditions for it and it is necessary to focus on creating an environment. The idea of the third renaissance is close to our national psyche and the dreams of our people. The people already want the river that flowed before to flow again. Any great plans, great ideas will gain vitality and reality only if they are directly connected with human needs, renewal of life, increase in freedom and spiritual maturity. Otherwise, it will remain as a fantasy. Therefore, each of us should feel from the bottom of our hearts that we are participants of the third renaissance.

References:

1. Address of the President of the Republic of Uzbekistan Sh. Mirziyoyev to the Oliy Majlis. People's word. December 30, 2020. #276. Page 2.
2. Renan "Dialogues fragments philosophic" – "philosophical dialogues and fragments". F., 1876, p. VIII-IX.
3. Encyclopedia of World Philosophy Publishing House "National Society of Philosophers of Uzbekistan". Tashkent-1916, volume 2, page 510.
4. Spiritual stars. Responsible editor: M.M. Khairullaev. T:A. Qadiri publishing house of folk heritage, 1999, p. 321
5. https://xs.uz

Alkaloids

Abstract
Nitrogen- containing heterocyclic bases found in plants and having a strong physiological effect are called alkaloids. The term alkaloid, proposed by the pharmacist V. Meisner, means "alkaline". Alkaloids are nitrogenous organic compounds that are found in plants, rarely in animals, and have basic properties. Many alkaloids are nitrogen atoms are part of a ring of atoms, often called a ring system. The name of alkaloids usually ends with the suffix "-ina", which refers to their chemical classification as amines. Regardless of the role of alkaloids in plants, many alkaloids are used in human medicine. Alkaloids are produced by some living organisms, especially plants. However, the role of these molecules in plants has not been fully studied.
Keyword: biosynthesis, tropane and nicotine alkaloids, benzylisoquinoline   alkaloid,   protoalkaliods, pseudoalkaloids.

Introduction
Alkaloids are found as separate molecules, so they can absorb small and hydrogen ions and turn them into bases. The chemical structure of alkaloids is extremely variable. Usually, an alkaloid contains at least one nitrogen atom in an amine-like structure, that is, by replacing hydrogen atoms with hydrogen-carbon groups called hydrocarbons, ammonia derivative. This or another nitrogen atom can be active as a base in acid-base reactions. The name alkaloid was originally applied to these substances, because, like inorganic alkalis, they react with acids and form salts.
Alkaloid biosynthesis in plants involves many metabolic steps, catalyzed by enzymes belonging to the family of proteins, so the pathways of alkaloid biosynthesis are

45

quite complex. However, some generalities can be explained. There are several major branches in alkaloid synthesis, for example, the biosynthesis of tropane and nicotine alkaloids.

Methodology
Biosynthesis of tropane and nicotine alkaloids.
In this group of alkaloids, biosynthesis is carried out from compounds L-argine and ornithine. They undergo decarboxylation by means of their respective enzymes: arginine decarboxylase and ornithine decarboxylase. The product of this reaction is putrescine molecules. After other steps, including methyl groups transfer, nicotine derivatives and tropane derivatives are produced. Benzylisoquinline alkaloid biosynthesis. The synthesis of benzyl isoquinoline alkaloids begins with L-triosine molecules, which are decarboxylated by the enzyme triosine decarboxylase to form tyramine molecules. These enter into a series of complex reactions to form berberine, morphine and codeine alkaloids.
Due to the diversity and complexity of the structure, alkaloids can be classified in different ways. According to the biosynthetic origin of alkaloids, they are divided into three large groups:
- True alkaloids
- Protoalkaloids
- Pseudalkaloids

True alkaloids are those that are derived from amino acids and have a nitrogen atom that is part of a heterocyclic ring. For example: hygrin, caquine, physostigmine.
Protoalkaloids are derived from amino acids, but nitrogen is not part of the heterocyclic ring. For example: ephedrine, calchicine.
Pseudoalkaloids are alkaloids that are not derived from amino acids and nitrogen is part of the heterocyclic

structure. For example: aconitine (terpenic alkaloid) and solanidine (steroidal alkaloid).

Alkaloids have several uses and applications in nature and in society. The use of alkaloids in nature is based on their physiological effects on the body, which is a measure of the toxicity of the compound. Alkaloids are organic molecules produced by living organisms. Has the structural ability to interact with biological systems and directly affects the physiology of the organism. This property may seem dangerous, but the use of alkaloids in a controlled way is very useful. Despite their toxicity, some alkaloids are it is useful when used in large doses. Excessive doses are harmful and toxic to the body. Alkaloids are mainly obtained from shrubs and herbs. They are found in various parts of plants, such as leaves, stems, roots, etc.

Alkaloids can be used as medicine.

Some alkaloids have significant pharmacological activity. These physiological effects are used as medicine to treat some serious diseases. For example: vincristine from Vinca roseus is used as an anticancer drug and ephedrine is used as an anti- cancer drug, Ephedra dystachya is used to regulate blood pressure, cadein-used to suppress cough. Alkaloids contain drugs. Many psychotropic substances that affect the central nervous system are contained in alkaloids. For example, opium morphine is used as a medicine and pain reliever. This drug has been used as a means of mental excitement since ancient times, but according to modern medicine is harmful.

Alkaloids are also used as pesticides.

Most natural pesticides and repellants are derived from plants, where they act as part of the plant's defense system against insects, fungi, or bacteria that attack them. These compounds are often alkaloids. As mentioned above, these alkaloids are toxic in nature. Although this property is highly dependent on concentration. For example, pyrethrin is used as an insecticide, which is dangerous for mosquitoes, but not dangerous for humans. Alkaloids are used in scientific research centers.

Conclusion

Alkaloids are used in scientific research due to their specific effects on the body. Some alkaloids are studied with great interest due to their antitumor properties, for example, vinblastine and reserpine, among others. Therefore, alkaloids should be used for the right purpose.

References:

1. Kordel. G (2003) Alkaloids: Chemistry and Biology, Volume 60 (1st Edition)
2. Venkert.E (1959). Alkaloid biosynthesis.
3. Mirxamidova.P., Boboxonkva D., Zikriyayev A. "Biologik kimyo va molekulyar biologiya" 1-qism. Toshkent- 2018. 110-111.
4. Anna Kampa. "Peroxidases Chemistry and Biology" Volume II 2.25 pages.1991. books.google.com.
   Internet networks used:
5. https://uz.warbletoncouncil.org
6. https://ziyonet.uz

Bahara Shodmonkulova daughter of Ilhom, was born on June 23, 2010 in Gallaorol district of Jizzakh region. Currently, he is a 7th grade student of the 42nd school.

My future
White and spotless as the clouds,
I have my dreams.
Fortune is always with me,
All my dreams will surely come true.

The passion deep inside me-
Never will fade away.
The faith of my country's leader,
Will always be a beacon in my way!

Abdulazizova Sabina Husan's daughter was born on February 2, 2007 in Uychi district of Namangan region. Currently, she is studying in the 9th grade of the 26th school in the district.

Life
When I leave life and the world,
If I don't hold flowers in your hands.
Don't b offended, take my head,
If I pour out like a spring and don't flow back.

Well, don't remember, don't be sad,
They say "he is no longer in the world".
Look up at the sky and smile softly,
Say: "Dreams are enough today".

If my soul turns into a butterfly,
I come to you every day, you know.
Don't even look at your face,
If your daughter forgets like me.

Toshmurodova Muhayyo Isomiddin's daughter was born in Jizzakh region, Gallaorol district on 13th September, 1984. Currently she is a working as a youth leader in 1st vocational school in Gallaorol.

Thankful

You have achieved the day that your grandfathers dreamed of,
You have reached the year that your grandmothers intended.
Don't stop learning the history of your ancestors,
Be thankful for every morning that given as a present.

Fortunately, the sun always illuminates the earth,
And the rays are quietly spread around.
Even the rain is suddenly poured,
Be thankful for every morning that given as a present.

When stones roll from the mountains,
Girls pick up tulips and sing songs.
Children return from the mountain with joy,
Be thankful for every morning that given as a present.

Try hard to help all the needy orphans,
So that you can see their happiness.
Don't be jealous of your trail,
Be thankful for every morning that given as a present.
If your property is stolen by this,
Don't be confused and don't have stress.
If you honestly live and you don't cheat,
Be thankful for every morning that given as a present.

Abbosova Iroda Otabek daughter was born in 2006 in Jizzakh region in Gallaorol district. Now she is a student of 1st vocational shool in Gallaorol.

Spring

Spring! All the hearts are impatiently waiting for you,
You are the beautiful season of every country.
Your charm attracts everyone in the lands,
And you are the real origin of beauty.

You are silently ashamed like a bride,
Red tulips calmly open their leaves.
Every morning dew falls to the ground,
And it is scattered in all directions.

Spring! Why are such an elegant season,
When I touch your flowers, they drop their petals.
After I shed your priceless beauty,
My heart is suddenly filled with bad emotions.

Dear spring, never stop flourishing,
Always share your beauty to the land.
Come and stay often in four seasons,
And don't make people feel sad.

Berdiyorova Durdona Qahramon's daughter was born 28th November, 2006 in Jizzakh region, Gallaorol district. Currently she is a studying at 1st vocational school in Gallaorol.

My loving and affectionate mother
When I was sick, she did not sleep all night,
And asked God to heal my health disorder.
She has never showed her sorrow to anyone,
She is my loving and affectionate mother.

She endured the shortage as she can,
Inside of her heart is full of pain.
I know she cried at night like rain,
She is my loving and affectionate mother.

She has always put on old clothes,
So that we buy garments which are better.
And she didn't stop working to feed us,
She is my loving and affectionate mother.
You may see early wrinkles on her face,
And disappointment covered her eyes.
Life folded her dignity because of us,
She is my loving and affectionate mother.

Tohirova Maftunakhan Zakirjon was born on January 20, 1994 in Fergana region of the Republic of Uzbekistan and is currently a third-year student of Fergana State University.

Pursue knowledge, learn science!
The spring of life is in season of youth,
In a beautiful garden covered with flowers.
At the first dawn of the night before his arrival,
Pursue the knowledge, learn the science.

Acquiring knowledge is equal to prayer,
A man of knowledge will have a broad temper.
Be careful to your mortal and the eternal life,
Pursue the knowledge, learn the science!

Science shines a light in the darkness,
Removes the shackles of ignorance.
Brings enlightenment to every soul,
Pursue the knowledge, learn the science!
Be Bukhari and Navoi in science,
Be Ibn Sina, Ulugbek, Farabi in the life.
Be a perfect person in seeking only good,
Pursue the knowledge, learn the science!

Going slow from bad to good,
Happiness, luck are free for learned.
Knowledge is a gift from God to a servant,
Pursue the knowledge, learn science!

Gulrukhsor Tokhirjonova was born on November 12, 2005 in the Beruniy district of the Republic of Karakalpakstan. Founder of the girl's academy "Inspire yourself". Asih Sasami of Indonesia, a member of Juntos por las letras Writers Union of Argentina, All Indian Council for Technical Skill Development of India, Iqra Foundation of Pakistan.

Brave and courageous
People create their own destiny.

(Paulo Coelho)
I would like to start my speech by introducing successful girls who are known to you and recognized by the whole world.

1. Gigi Hadid was recognized as "the best model of the year" at the age of 21.
2. Malala won the Nobel Prize at the age of 17.
3. Charlie Damelio became the "Queen of Tik Tok " with 101 million followers on the Tik Tok network.
4. Emma Watson became famous for the role of Hermione at the age of 11 time, she won 5 Grammy Awards
5. Billie Eilish became "world domination" at the age of 18. At the same.
6. Madison Beer released her world-famous album at the age of 17.
7. Greata Thunberg became known to the world as a "Social Activist" at the age of 16 when she spoke at the UN about environmental issues and climate change.

Now ask yourself a question. How old are you it has nothing to do with age, what you have admired so far. Give yourself an objective assessment from the outside.

Eve some of us do not have an independent opinion. There are those who are afraid to go to the store at the beginning of the street alone. As long as your peers are studying alone in such and such a country. If you want to buy clothes, you either go with your mother, or rely on your friend's opinion, and ask someone on the phone every step of the way. Because you don't trust yourself completely yet or you are so dependent on your mother. No it's time to grow up dear. You have to make your own decisions. Allow yourself to do it! Maybe you have dreams and you are afraid that your parents and family will not understand. Do you force yourself that I should study in the university they want, work in the job they like? Then will this make their dreams come true? What about you? You barely finish a field you don't love, and then you start working without loving your profession. No matter how hard you try, you can't do well in a job you don't love. By doing this, you will harm the society and yourself. Just don't be afraid, be bold. (I will give an example as a profession) Fight for your favorite profession, career. Be able to prove to those around you that you feel happy too. "You'll never achieve your dreams unless you seize them. If you don't ask, you won't get answers. If you don't move forward, you'll stay where you are".

Jamoliddinova Mumtozbegim was born on April 20, 2002 in Uychi district of Namangan region. Currently, she is a 2nd-year student of the Uzbek language department at the Faculty of Philology of Namangan State University.

A dream
Chasing the wind and playing,
I want to sleep on a cloud always.
In emoticons bright smiling,
I want to be the sun all days.

Even if I become a friend with the moon,
If I tell my secret to the moon.
Even if our lives are together,
The most beautiful girl of mine forever.

Glowing brightly always,
I wish there was lightning in the eyes.
If I were a star, smiling in the sky,
Called over the distant sky.

With taking necklaces to nature,
I wish it was raining by the sky.
Giving beauty to the world,
I flowed down from the sky.

Choriyeva Komila Norkuchkor's daughter was born on 2003 in Langar- ota village, Qamashi district, Kashkadarya region. Currently, he is studying at Bukhara State University in the 1st stage.

In memory of our first president Islam Karimov

My countryman, your name is an epic in languages,
You are the reason why Uzbekistan lived.
You became independent from the former council,
You created for us forever garden.

So that my people can play and laugh without suffering,
You didn't find peace on your own.
My dream is the burden on my shoulders,
I couldn't thank you enough.

We, the youth, will continue on your way,
Uzbekistan is still a great future.
We believe in you, and your soul rejoices,
After all, we have a great future.

We are growing up to understand you now,
Without hitting our heads on hard rocks.
I pray to God every day,
My heaven bless you, our first president.

Sattorova Hulkaroy Kashkadarya region, Kokdala district 6th general secondary school, 8th "A" grade student.

Navoi's poetry

"Khamsa" spread Turkic to the world,
"Mahbub ul-Qulub" is dear to our hearts.
Dedicating gazelle to the language,
Let the creator's wish come true.

The gazelle is touching,
This is generosity of creativity and talent.
Pure feelings fill the heart,
This is the refreshment of our generous grandfather.

The truth is, the darkness is filled with light,
I was surprised by Mirkarim Osim.
Every line of Navoi's tunes,
His passion is in the song… in the song.

Poetry… it's a spell that fills my mind,
It's a golden lesson to grow old.
My heart is filled with magic,
Poem and song of my grandfather Navoi.

Gulrang Jabborova Fakhriddin daughter was born on April 10, 2004 in Shofirkon district, Bukhara region. She is a participant of "Parvoz youth forum", "Unity forum", "21st century is our century" forum.

A bitter memory

When this incident happened, I was about 14 years old. I was a girl full of dreams, who wanted to speak for hours on big stages. One day, the leader of our school read an announcement for a new competition. Then I thought that I would participate in this competition and I would win. I said and fulfilled the necessary conditions. I began to prepare for the competition very hard. The days passed and finally the day I was waiting for came. I was very excited. The day of the competition coincided with my class day. I explained to my teachers that it was a competition and asked for permission. It was on this day that luck smiled so much that I won the 1st place and qualified for the Republican stage. I came home, my father and mother congratulated everyone, it was a real celebration in our house. I was surprised. The teacher said: "Gulrang can't get a place anyway, she just likes to pass the time and avoid class. We'll see how far she goes." Then something broke inside me. I didn't know if it was sweet feelings about people, about my teachers, about my beloved school. I came home without saying a word. The next morning, I deliberately went to school late. At that time, the morning assembly at our school did not spread even though I was late for some reason. I said, "I think I will hear something again" The most painful thing was, he said on my forehead: "We knew that you have knowledge. If we set an example for everyone, we will respect you." I felt then... there are still many such situations. I wonder if there is a law in our Constitution that says you should be a hypocrite, I didn't know...

Makhamova Charos was born on December 23, 2005 in the Orta Chirchik district of the Tashkent region of the Republic of Uzbekistan. He studies in the 11th grade of school 44 in Orta Chirchik district.

Father

When we hear this word, the first thing that comes to our mind is the shield person who protects us from all dangers in our life. Our father loves us not from the time we are in our mother's body, tolerates our stubbornness, provides us with things. Even after we have passed the age of adulthood, he protects us and forgives us no matter how many mistakes we make. They give us everything they have, and we only call them father. Because of our father's presence, we walk freely in the streets. Because they are our shield.

In my opinion, father's love for their children is true love. Let us cherish our fathers in life. Let's say our sweet words in life, and after they die, we write these sweet words for a penny. I also try to be a person who always thanks my father. Our parents work early and late so that we can grow up, study, and walk like no other. Fathers give their children a lot. And even if we unknowingly hurt their hearts, they will not be offended by us. There are people who say, "I hate my father, because he has no money, or my father is blind, my father is blind". In fact, the hearts of these children are blind. Even if the father is poor, his health is real wealth, even if the father is disabled, his heart is beating, he is giving love to his child, he loves his child. But there are children who carry their father on their head. He thanks his father everywhere. We thank God when we see such children. There is a saying in our people that "Father is pleased- Allah is pleased." If we are loving, intelligent, well-educated, believing people, if we always thank our father, our father will be pleased with us. In order for us to be educated children, our father must be the head of the family. If our mother respects our father, if the father has a place in the family, then the children will have the same love for the father. Especially, the love of a girl child for her father will be different. Maybe because the girl child is considered the honor and face of her father, maybe because the girl child id a guest in her father's house. The more we talk about fathers, the less we can say... It is worth writing a novel about them. Because paper and pen are too weak to describe them. Fathers are the manifestation of love and affection in human form. I would say to everyone, appreciate your fathers, no one can give the love they gave to you.

Today I want to say something I rarely say to my father: Dad, I love you!

Marjona Asadova is the daughter of **Akmal.** She was born in Kitab district, Kashkadarya region. She graduated from school with the "Gold Medal"in 2020. Student of Shahrisabz State Pedagogical Institute.

Shame...

Yasmina is in the 8th grade of the school. She is the first among her classmates to wear the latest fashion clothes. All her classmates look at her with envy. Yasmina, noticing this, always brags to her classmates that they say that I am the only girl whose father is a big businessman.
One day, around late hour food was served on the table.
Father: Call our daughter, who has a mother, the food will get cold. Let her eat quickly, then she will do her lesson.
Mother: it's okay, now daddy!
My daughter. Yasmina, my daughter go out to eat soon...
Yasmina: Uf, what to eat?!
Mother: I fried pasta that you like, daughter!!!
Yasmina furrowed her brows, came to the table and said- "Don't look at pasta, pasta. Like people, when do we eat better food, or when do we go to restaurants".
Mother: What do you mean, my daughter? The food is not good or bad. Some people don't even have that. Yesterday was my friend Sarvinoz's birthday.
He didn't even look at the two books I gave him. Because, compared to the gifts given by my other classmates, mine is not worth the price. His father gave him the latest phone. As for me, what do I lack from him?
It's all your fault. I also want to celebrate my birthday in a beautiful way. I am ashamed to let them into this house with a crooked roof. My classmates' parents work in high positions. What about me? Do you know what will happen if my mother is a janitor and my father is a guard???
Everyone laughs at me. As if that wasn't enough, what I did that day didn't crack the ground and I didn't go into

the ground. I'm tired of telling you this a thousand times. Fortunately, I have only one daughter and one child. Why did you give birth to me, if you can't fulfill my need.

When Yasmina said these words, she closed the door and went into her room crying…

His father and mother looked at each other for a long time and became silent.

Father: Where did we go astray, where did we make a mistake? Is it our fault that we ate without eating, or that we wore without wearing?

Mother: Don't worry, dad is still young. He talks without thinking.

When his mother said these words, tears filled her eyes and she went out to the kitchen saying that she would come to renew the tea.

To be continued…

Kholmuradova Sevinch Ulugbek daughter was born on June 17, 2004 in Kashkadarya. She is a student of the 2nd stage of the Uzbek National Music Art Institute named after Yunus Rajabi.

Childhood

I always remember my childhood,
I look for joy in my dreams.
The day I played on the sand,
I laughed without worry.

I remembered my tears of joy,
My days passed like a fairy tale.
My eyes are searching for my childhood,
My heart tells me to grow up.

Sometimes I wonder,
What do I look for in my past tears.
I look to the future,
I will keep my childhood forever.

Dilorom Tokhatabayeva was born on November 1, 2006 in Turtkul district of the Republic of Karakalpastan, 1st place winner or the district stage of reading competrions and the regional stage of "Science Olympiad- 2022"

Mulberry memories
"Everyone's birthplace is he city of Egypt"

(Proverb)
Every time he goes to his village, he goes to the trap located near his yard. It was the same today. As he walked around catch, memories of him began to flood his mind. After returning from school, he still remembers how he ran to the mulberry tree with his brother and his aunt's daughter and ate the huge white and black mulberries hanging from the branches. He remembers the times when his lips and cheeks were painted red, he was nicknamed "street child". Oh, what and innocent childhood.

He still remembers. At that time, Sadiq was studying in the 7th grade. When she was eating mulberries at noon with her neighbor Umida, she heard a scolding from her mother.

- Hey, girl, don't fall! What are your brother? He hangs on my leg and won't stop using me.

Let your father come, I will tell you. I will never see you with this boy again. A fourteen-year-old girl. (Mother Saida did not like Sadiq for some reason)

- Mom now!- Umida began to cry as if to go home.

At the same time, Umida stopped eating mulberries. And Sadiq knew that the girl likes mulberries very much. One day he filled a bowe with the finest mulberries and whistled in the courtyard of the Umida's. A boy ran out of them without pants. It was Umida's four- year- old brother Bakhtiyar.

- Oh, catch it? Give to me too- he said, pointing to the bowe and tasting it.
- If your call your sister, I will kiss you with a mulberry, Sadiq smiled and winked. The boy was clapping his hands and laughing. At that moment, Umida's sonorous voice was heard from inside:
- Bakhtiyar, who is he? Why are you laughing.
- Hope, I brought it. After a while, Umida came out of the house. "Thank you," said the girl, shyly taking the bowe full of mulberries from his hand. His brother made a mistake and put a zap on the mulberry in Umida's hand. And Sadiq was overjoyed to have the girl as his guest.

He tured into a parrot street on his old bicycle.

When he remembers the memories of Umida like this, his heart sinks. The poor girl had already become a bride for Shakir to the carpenter at the age twenty. When she was in the prime of her your. Sadiq is currently studying in the 3 year. There are many tall, luxurious buildings in Tashkent, but nowhere can compare to the spacious courtyard in the village where he was born and raised. After all, he had a happy child hood there.

Time has passed. It was very hot. Mulberry cake. When he came to village of sweetheart, he went directly of catch from those dear paths. Children, big and small, were licking their fingers and eating mulberries in the place that was dear to Sadiq. The memories of the mulberry began to come to life in front of his eyes: Umida, the brother who ran without pants, etc.

Suddenly, Sadiq's attention was drawn to the fact that a boy in the 3rd grade was bending tree branches to pick up mulberries.

- My brother, take care of him! He called the boy to him and explained how many children should be left with these tusks.
- News, recently his first book was published: Sadiq Samandarov "Memories of Mulberry". Although, it is not surprising that childhood moments held a pencil in his hand for the first time.

Sevara Eshonkulova, a third-year student of the Faculty of Journalism of the Karakalpak State University. She is the author or the book "Mysterious World".

"The land watered with blood"

My mother tells the stories of the pharaohs. – This, Pharaoh, who claims to be a god to his people, ordered the Muslim maid to be thrown alive into a huge boiling cauldron. My mother has a bad habit. If I don't wash the dishes on time during the day, if I don't pretend to make the house as clean as sheet she stops at the most interesting part of the story telling time and punish us without continuing. Maybe because of the war period, in the countryside where we live, there were no people who considered themselves rich. The thatched walls, which were leaning on the ground, were ready to give their bosom to the soil, using the lying wind as an excuse. The last crops of the villagers, who were waiting for the harvest, were robbed, and the whole nation was left without wheat. I still can't forget those years. My mother's shoelaces were worn out. She didn't wear it regularly, she only used it do walk along the thorny, thick sand road to visit my grandmother's grave. Kindhearted mother baked bread from a light bag of wheat that she kept in the barn, and took it out sometimes to aunt Salima's house. One day, a young man, who is either familiar or unfamiliar to my mother, and a complete stranger to me, begged my mother to give him slippers for his mother, whose foot was swollen with pus. On the one hand, my mother's right hand, who was feeling pity, was handing out shoes, and on the other hand, her left hand was trying to return the gift, saying, "If you walk barefoot on that thorny path, your feet will be no different from hers"... The land that was watered with the blood that leaked from my mother's blessed steps, and where the cypress sprouted, today has been turned into a royal garden with marble stones. There is a race of people who can't be indifferent to the golden counter. It says: "This road is dedicated to the memory of a generous woman named Noila".

Davron Navodir Rakhmonovich was born on May 29, 2003 in Kitab district of Kashkadarya region. Currently a student of Tashkent State Transport University. To date, he has participated in more than 30 international symposiums, forums, conferences and festivals, and has more than 15 scientific articles.

The writer of two nations
This fight is for the law of life,
This lamp is for the end of life.

(Maksud Sheikzade)
One of the famous representatives of Uzbek literature, famous poet, great playwright, literary scholar and translator Maksud Sheikzade was born in 1908 in the city of Aktash, Azerbaijan. After receiving primary and secondary education in Aktash, he studied part-time at the Baku Higher Pedagogical Institute, and from 1925 he worked as a teacher in Darband. Sheikzade came to Tashkent in 1928, worked in the editorial offices of various newspaper and magazines, and 1935-1938 was a researcher at the Institute of Language and Literature under the Committee of Sciences,, from 1938 until the end of his life at the Department of Uzbek Classical Literature of the Nizamiy Tashkent State Pedagogical Institute (now the university) served as an associate professor and participated in the training of highly qualified personnel. The literary activity of the poet began in 1929. The publication of his collections "O'n she'r" (1932), "Undoshlarim" (1933), "Uchinchi kitob" (1934), "Jumhuriyat" (1934) signaled that a poet with a unique voice was entering literature.
In the tragedy "Laloliddin Manguberdi" (1944), written by Sheikzade during the Second World War, he described the fighting courage of the last Khorezm king who fought

against the Mongol invaders for the freedom and independence of his country. During these years, the poet mobilized all his creative energy and warmth of his heart for the victory over the enemy. From the first days of the war, "Kurash nechun" (1942), "Jang va qo'shiq" (1942), "Ko'ngil deydiki..." historical drama "Jaloliddin Manguberdi" (1944) and a number of other journalistic works were published. In the years after the war, Maksud Sheikzade created poetry collections about the struggle for peace, such as "O'n bech yilning daftari", "Olqishlarim", "Zamon torlari", "Shu'la" and "Chorak asr devoni". Poet was not spared from the oppression of the authoritarian regime. He was imprisoned for the first time in 1928 and was accused of anti-Soviet propaganda and exiled to Uzbekistan for 3 years. The second time, Sheikzade was expelled from the Union of Writers of Uzbekistan, imprisoned on September 22, 1952 and deprived of freedom for 25 years.

The poet was relased after Stalin's death: returned to creativity and in 1958 wrote the lyric epic "Toshkentnoma" dedicated to the old and modern city of Tashkent. In 1960, he wrote the tragedy "Mirzo Ulugbek", in which he created and enlightened statesman Mirzo Ulugbek. Sheikzade translated Pushkin's "Mis chavandoz" , Lermontov's "Kavkaz asiri", Mayakovsky's "Juda soz" and many poems, Shakespeare's tragedies and sonnets "Hamlet", "Romeo and Juliet", Nazim Hikmat's poems, works of Azerbaijan poets into Uzbek. In his poetry, Sheikzade used his pen mainly on modern themes, and his dramaturgy, he took a deep look at the historical past and gave a new artistic life to figures and events that help to illuminate modern problems in it. In the last years of his life, he wrote his last play about Beruni.

Sheikzade's scientific work on the history of Uzbek literature, Uzbek folk art, in particular, the research of

Alisher Navoi's work is also commendable. Sheikzade not only wrote works in all types and genres of artistic creation, but also worked effectively as a literary critic and critic. As early as 1941, Sheikzade until the last days of his life, he was constantly engaged in Navoi's life and work. After the article "Navoiyning lirik qahramoni haqida" (1948), which he wrote on the occasion of Navoi's 500th anniversary, "Navoiy lirikasining ba'zi bir poetik usullari haqida" (1959), "Ustodning san'atxonasida" (3-part article, 1965-1966), "G'azal mulkining sultoni" (1966), "Tazkirachilik tarixidan" (1968), created major scientific studies, and brought the science of narcotics to a new stage of development. The poet died in 1967 in Tashkent.

Conclusion
Maqsud Sheikzade was a candidate of philological sciences and an associate professor. But above all, he was a great poet. The writer's works have been translated into the languages of many neighboring and foreign nations. In 2001, Sheikzade was awarded the Order of Merit for his great contribution to the development of Uzbek literature and culture.

References:
1. https://sirlar.uz/maqsud-shayxzoda-1908-1967-haqida-batafsil-ma-lumotlar-tarjimai-hol
2. https://kh-davron.uz/kutubxona/uzbek/memuarlar/maqsud-shayxzoda-haqida-xotiralar.html
3. "Maqsud Sheikzade"- Naim Karimov, Tashkent 2018.

Lola Khamdamova, daughter of **Olimjon** was born on March 8, 1997 in Kamashi district, Kashkadarya region. Currently, she is a student of Tashkent State Transport University. Lola has participated in more than 100 international symposiums, forums, conference and festivals, has more than 50 scientific articles, and is a member of UZLiDeP.

Maksud Sheikzade
Each person leaves in them or a solid house built to last.

The famous poet and writer Maksud Sheikzade was born in 1908 in Azerbaijan in the city Agdash (Aktash), which was located in the Ganja region.

He began writing poetry at a young age. He admits: "I started writing poetry before mastering the alphabet." The first examples of creativity were created in his homeland, but because of his advanced ideas, he was repressed and moved to Tashkent in 1929. From then until the end of his days, Uzbekistan became his second home. In Tashkent, the poet begins work in newspaper and magazines, teaches at higher educational institutions, including scientific activities at the Nizami State Pedagogical University. Many of his studies played an important role and contributed to the development of Uzbek literature. The contribution of Maksud Sheikzade to Uzbek literature adequately appreciated by the government of independent Uzbekistan. A number of schools and streets named after him. Maksud Sheikzade also awarded the Order of Merit in 2001. The poet never explored book problems. He, above all, paid attention to issues that he himself was impressed and inspired by. The words of the poet awaken fires in the heart of the reader in his poems, especially beautiful artistic images. For the poet, sometimes a boat at sea seems to be "a spot on the water", and the tail of a seagull expressed as "A question on the horizon". The prince's poems "For a quarter of a century", "The world is eternal", "Alley" were published in dozens of collections. Since these poems are full of high human dreams, they were sung with love, pain and hope. For forty years of his work, Sheikzade sang about Lenin, and about the Kremlin, and about the Soviet. But the value of his poetry lies not in works of this direction, but in works that, revealing the intricacies of the human heart and unique states of the soul, enrich the wonderful moments in the life of the reader. Sheikzade believed that the main task of the poet is "The upbringing of the human spirit, goodness, a sense of beauty and sophistication at a high level". Toward the end of his life, Sheikzade experienced severe changes in his worldview and a series of losses in the outer and inner world of the poet. In 1966, Maksud's close friend , the great poet Gofur Gulam, and the great statesman who was close to the poet, Usman Yusupov, died. These losses echoed in the heart of the poet: "Forgiveness letter" and "Separation" (in memory of Usmon Yusupov). Respect for a person, artistic disclosure of the leading direction of Sheikzade's poetry. The poet himself met a lot of injustice during his life. In the 1920s, the poet met with unfair persecution, and in the early 50s he was imprisoned. Of course, this didn't last long. This poetic thought was more deeply revealed in the poem "Separation". Although the work was aimed at glorifying the memory of the beloved son of the people, the leader of Uzbekistan in the middle of the 20th century, in essence it revealed a sense of selflessness and patriotism. "The heart is small, but it can contain anything. It hurts to endure separation from a friend, and to contain in the heart the loss of the beloved son of the people," says the poet, "The size of mourning is immeasurable, Bitter cries in the chest". Maksud

Sheikhzade enriched Uzbek literature with historical dramas Jaloliddin Manguberdi and Mirzo Ulugbek. Sheikzade played a major role in translating the works of Shakespeare, Byron, Maksmumkili, Tagore, Avetik Isahakyan and Nozim Hikmat.

References:
1. Shomansur Yu. Sheikzade: Literary-critical essay.-Tashkent 1969.
2. Sandjar Sadikov- "textbook for students of the faculties of philology and journalism of higher educational institutions" Tashkent 2003.
3. https://arboblar.uz
4. https://library.ziyonet.uz

Munavvar Boltayeva Yusuf daughter was born in 1997 in Sukhandarya region. She is student of the 1st stage of elementary educational at Renaissance education a University.

ARTEL village of Surkhandarya?

ARTEL village of Surkhandarya?! Yes, no water should be opened in corner of our country, surely these waters will be involuntarily swallowed by our tongues, Surkhandarya, a beautiful land, has been known since time immemorial as an oasis of Alpomish, world-recognized Termizites and thinkers. During the years of independence, our province has become more beautiful than before. In particular, those who have visited the Jarkurgan district feel a big difference comparing its night and day. Now our district is becoming prosperous and magnificent. The streets have become smoother, modern buildings are rising around them. The formation of our villages on the basis of the houses in the project, the concern of our honorable President and the government regarding the welfare of the family, the upbringing of a healthy and well-rounded generation, revives feelings of great pride in our hearts. Big buildings, beautiful buildings, high-rise residences, and sports complexes are being built in our district. Seeing such changes, the hands of our elders will certainly be opened to prayer. All of us are proud to be the children of such a country with smooth streets and all facilities. "904 boys and girls are regularly engaged in volleyball, basketball, handball, mini football, sports gymnastics, wrestling, taekwondo, boxing, judo, rhythmic gymnastics in sports school no. 6 for children and teenagers in the district." Our youth have been showing themselves in various sports. He is raising the flag of our country even higher by going too countries like Turkey, Azerbaijan and Russia. Even the parents of these young people come to the gym and do sports in their free time. This is really gratifying, because we adults should be an example for a healthy generation" says the director of the sports school. Nazokat Javlieva: a woman from "Istiklol" neighborhood – "774 families and 3047 people live in 455 houses in our neighborhood. The population of our territory is engaged in animal husbandry and farming. Also, 18 houses have greenhouses, they supply crops such as tomatoes and cucumbers even in the frosty days of winter and provide food for the residents. 11 households prepare tandir gusht. They even come from far and wide to eat from our village's ovens. "Istiklol" neighborhood is divided into several villages. Among them is the ARTEL village, which I am about to write about. To be honest, I was very surprised when I asked our elders. Artel village was founded in 1930-1931. Its history goes back to previous years. The old people who managed the village of Artel at that time, and even their children, have left this world. But I will try to write all information that I can. Artel is one of the forms of voluntary association of citizens for the purpose of joint execution of production processes (fishing, agricultural artels) or to associations that combine the ownership of the means of production, without generalizing the production of the members. From the beginning of the 20s, the farms of individual producers of goods (artisans, artisans and other) engaged in labor activities in the former Union were transferred to the socialist economy based on the generalization of the means of production. Collective farms, such as village farms, handicrafts, fishing ARTELLAS, were established. Their production plans were included in the national economic plan. At the end of 1980s, when the laws on individual cocktail activities were adopted, such ARTELS ceased to exist. But our village of ARTELLAS still survived. People's hearts were happy and their hearts were happy every household of Jarkurgan. A country where the hearts are happy and the hearts are prosperous will always rise and develop. Seeing this, our mothers and fathers are always thankful for their creation and open their hands in prayer so as not to disturb our peace. They show us what they have seen in the past and encourage us to value peace. They ask me everywhere I golf I ask which village of Zharkurgan you are from, and answer "Tandir from the village", they will curiously ask if they make tandoor in your village. But our village is famous not for making tandoors, but for tandoori kebabs. A few years ago, our village was visited by guests from "My peer in the village" on the TV channel "Yoshlar". We were very happy about it, the heads of the villagers went to the sky. When I introduced "Tandir village", they were surprised by everything I said and rushed to get to know the villagers. Our village has existed for a long time, and its previous name was "Tuyakush". Many people wondered why exactly "Tuyakush" because of this, the villagers raised camels. A few decades later, a large workshop was opened in the village. They called it 7 treasures. The workshop included a cotton mill, a carpet weaving workshop, a rice workshop, an electric welding (welding) workshop, a wood workshop (making doors and chests), a satin-silk weaving workshop and a flour mill. Therefore, these 7 treasure villages were named "Artel". Later, the carpet weaving workshop in Artel developed rapidly, and for some reasons, the work of other workshops slowed down a bit. From time to time, the cotton ginning workshop was strengthened and a new brick factory was built by the people. It would be possible to know that each shop is working well from a visitor coming from afar. The turnover of the carpet weaving workshop has increased considerably. In addition to patterns, carpets were also made famous by painting various pictures. I heard many times that my mother Feruza Ishmamedova woven the photo of sports commentator Akhbor Imomkhojaev into the carpet. In addition, the making seen in of chests was also started. Despite its small size, "ARTEL" village has started   activities in every field. We heard from our grandmothers and grandfathers that the villagers are very harmonious and live as one body and soul. The "Zang" canal was dug by the villagers of Totuv by means of earthworms, and we still use it widely to this day. The proof that Surkhandarya is land of wrestlers and Chopagon is a land of horsemen can be seen in the form of brave young men in the village. It seems that wrestling at weddings and horse- racing at goats have become a legend. But the simple villagers, who have not followed the traditions until now, still live with a sense of gratitude. Over the years, the development of the village has grown to another level as human thinking has grown. "Tandir kebab was prepared here for the first time and sold not in kitchens, but on streets, Surkhandarya and Kashkadarya roads. At that time, tandir meat was not very popular. For the first time, tandir kebab was prepared by the older generation in our village says the chairman of the neighborhood Bakhodir Turdaliev. "I have been the chairman of this community for many years. Our neighborhood is "Istiklol" neighborhood, which includes "Artel" ivided into several village. this village used to have manufacturing and we can still see it today. One farm is engaged in sewing, another one is engaged in animal husbandry, some have opened a bakery, some have opened a tea shop. We are certainly happy about this, because they are moving towards development, using all their capabilities". Bakhodir Turdialiev, the chairman of the "Istiklol"community assembly, said happily. Until now, restaurants such as "Zharkurgan tandir kabobi" or "Surkhandarya tandir kabobi" are operating in Termiz and other regions, as well as in the city of Tashkent. During the quarantine period in our country, my fellow villagers, who continued their activities online without types of delicious tandoori kebabs throughout our country. But they are not satisfied with kuzychok gusht, they also prepare delicious kebabs from chicken and chicken gusht. Surkhandarya tandoori kebabs, know all over the world, are made in our village. from this period until now, other kitchens have been strengthened. In the next 10 years, the village of "Artel" changed into the village of "Tandir" and has been operating in this way.

Rustamova Feruzabonu is the daughter of **Alisher.** She was born on September 25, 2008 in the Gijduvan district of the Bukhara region of the Republic of Uzbekistan. Currently studies at the first Specialized State General Education School.

Person is a wonderful torch
The most intelligent creature- person. Only person differs from other creature from his thinking. Man is the most noble of all created beings. "It's our life. Life is beautiful. We are capable of living a beautiful life. The reason is that we were born as "Humans" says the Turkish writer Mirach Chagri Aktash. Or let's take an example "The old man and sea" written by Ernest Hemingway, one of the favorite and cherished writer of children, it is the last work of the writer, Hemingway tries to show that the value of a person is greater than everything, and he wants to create a real old man, a real sea through the image of Santiago. By reading the book, one can understand that a person can believe in himself in any situation and achieve his goal with patience. Here it is impossible not to remember these words of the writer: "Person's greatest victory over himself". Indeed, person was created noble and honorable. Islam has raised the value of a person to such an extent that even the respect of the living and the dead is valued equally. As our people say "He who does not know his own value, does not know the value of others". HUMAN WORTH IS PRINCIPAL HONOR AND REPUTATION! What is most valuable thing for us? LIFE! The reason is that all our joys, all our happiness, all our hopes are connected only to with life. Life is more than reality. It is being able to paint and see the a world in different colors. Person is a miracle, life is beautiful!
Everyone understands these two concepts in their own way. As Anvar Obidjon said "Every moment of life is

beautiful, every part of life is a treasure". A person's life is priceless gift. It depends on us how to spend it. We rejoice in life's victories, we draw our own conclusions from failures and strive towards goals and achievements. At this point it is appropriate to remember the following words of Bulgakov: "Life consists of activity, and activity means struggle". Person should also understand that he is the Creator of his life own! Only the artist decides how to paint the picture. Person's humanity is not only to live, but also to live with peasure.

People are born, they grow up and pass away. But they don't live. If only we could add the word "live" in the phrase given above. Maybe then at lest. I would say "I lived my life" before dying.

Madaminova Husnidakhon, daughter of Ilhomjon, was born in 2007 in pepublic of Uzbekistan, Fergana region, Bagdad district, Churindi village. nowadays she is a student in 9th grade in 25th school.

Bread

I was a tiny child, three or four years old,
Curly hair, snub nose, dark eyebrows.
The dress I'm wearing has small stones,
I will never forget that moment.

When my mother sweats and bakes bread in the oven,
If he finds us in the streets.
When friends rush to my mother,
My soul is burned when I laugh and laugh.

I'm stubborn, my stubbornness is patient,
Add three or four kulcha to us.
I won the stubborn with a mother's love,
 Is my parikhan in front of my eyes.

We were happily running towards the river,
We used to cool the bread in water at that time.
And one day it was bad, very bad,
I couldn't hold it, my cake ran out.

Years passed, rushing like pomegranate water,
Sometimes joy and sometimes sadness.
Today the dream passed over me,
Every time I remember, my soul itches with pain.
This is my broken bread…

Shakhribonu Okmamatova Zafarjonovna was born on March 1, 2004. Student of University of World Economy and Diplomacy.

My contemporary peer!

Human life is like autumn, winter, spring, summer,
You taste food in independent land forever.
Swim towards the river of knowledge,
Break the ignorance against enlightenments.
Give up hope of living without a country,
Then your future will be the brightest.

My friend, my kind peer.
Share with your friends, I'm always remember here
Let's always remember our almighty grandfather.
Let's be a salve for shepherds' pain,
My Uzbek will never be less than other.
Let's go hand in hand,
Your future may not know grief in this land.

My friend, my sweat peer.
It's time to live well together,
Don't be fooled by lies.
Turn back from your ways,
 "Bow your head, bow, say thanks".

My friend, my faithful confidant!
My country is peaceful, my people are rich and my friend.
Let them live without knowing sorrow.
The long- awaited time has come now,
Our path is bright, a constant lamp tomorrow.
Let it bloom, let it live, this motherland
It's Uzbekistan, it's your friend.

Jurayeva Sabina daughter of **Barot**. She was born in Yangi Khayat neighborhood, Kogon district, Bukhara region. She is currently studying in the State Specialized Secondary School No1.

GLORIUS PAST
Theme: Uzbekistan is one of the diamond in the world.

As long there is a place where sunlight falls, of course, that place has its own history. How many sunny mornings and moonless, dark nights. Devoted peoples and unfaithful nations have passed in this past. In addition, the great history of my country, which is preserved in languages. Is still reflected in the historical buildings. Homeland is like a garden. The work and courage of s many gardeners has been absorbed into this garden. They were not just gardeners, they were the bloodshed for the country to achieve freedom. They were souls who sacrificed for the development of the country. They were the souls burned in the fire for the freedom of the Motherland. They are Amir Temur, Jalaluddin Manguberdi, Mirza Ulughbek, Zahiruddin Mohammed Babur, Alisher Navoi, Ibn Sina, Beruniy, Bukhariy, Khorezmiy, Termiziy, Zamakh Shariy…

They were Uzbek greats and rules. They were intellectuals who shook the whole world. One is a king and a post, the other is a ruler who was no equal in courage. One knows religion perfectly, and the whole Eurasia learned science from another. One is sultan in the property of gazelles, the other is an invincible, hero ruler. Their names are many and great. They were the first awakening, the first shining sun in the history of the whole world. They were renaissance recognized by the whole world. And we are the successors of this glory past, the authors of the new history book. We are the descendants of the great ones, the heirs of this holy land. Not only us, but also all the peoples of the world should have descendants like them of our ancestors. Now, unfortunately, the feeling of the Motherland has left many people, most of us are mired in a bottomless quagmire. But we must not forget that, Motherland is one! Only brave people can love and protect her. The future generation should mention our name along with the names of the ancestors of the past. We should be a brave, fair and noble person will the best for everyone. Our great ancestors and future generations should be proud of us. Let's be the generation worthy of our ancestors!!!

Orziyeva Gulchehra Elyor's daughter was born on July 22, 2007 in Kasbi district in Kashkadarya region. She si currently studying in the 9th grade at the 18th general secondary school in this district.

Is the internet good for us?

The 21st century is the era of advanced information technologies. Nowadays, international technologies are very effective for us. Perhaps, without these techniques, our efficiency would be very low. Information technology shortens distances and gives us many opportunities. For example: the possibility of communication and information exchange with different countries of the world. It is possible to apply to foreign universities and study at prestigious higher educational institutions through the online platform. Starting from the 2021 academic year, the remote evaluation system was launched in all regions of our Republic, that is, the "Kundalik.com" platform was launched.

What does the "Kundalik.com" platform give us? Avoiding Red Tape #1. The biggest advantage of this online diary is that the grades we receive at school are sent directly to the Ministry of Republic. Our 6-year grades are aggregated as a percentage and young people are given a discount for entering OTM. This is also a useful aspect of information technology! Thanks to the development of the Internet, there are also many social sites. There are many people who earn money doing business on such sites. If we look at it this way, technology will bring us many benefits and achievements. As they say, "there is another side to the coin", there is also a bad side to these sites.

The owners of our future should also use social networks. "What does the Internet really mean? " Translated from English (inter-entry, net-net) means "entry into the network". Our young people are browsing these social sites. What will this ultimately lead to? It serves to waste the time of the younger generation and, of course, poisons their minds but it's no secret their minds. But it's no secret that if the internet is used correctly, the scope of opportunities expands. There are many young people who use social networks correctly. However, my conclusion is that our young people study without wasting their lives, contribute to the development and growth of our country, and get rid of harmful vices, they will benefit both themselves and others!

Ochilova Marhabo Alisher's daughter was born on October 7, 2007 in Gulistan district, Syrdarya region. She is currently a 9th grade student of the 11th general secondary school.

Grandma
(Dedicated to my passed grandmother Niyozova Kunduz)
Caressing your face,
I want to hug you.
Grandma, where are you?
I want to see you.

You went, left us,
I can't find you, grandma.
I, your daughter, shivering,
I want to see you.

I still pray for you,
Every second every time.
Grandmother of my soul,
I want to hug you.